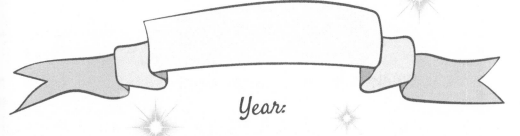

This book belongs to an awesome gymnast called:

Year:

Remember, everything you need to be great is already inside you

# Table of Contents

# About Me

Year _____ Age _____ Level _____

Club _____

Favorite Apparatus: _____

Best Apparatus: _____

Favorite move: _____

## Strengths:

Hard Worker ☐ Speed ☐ Strength ☐ Team Player

Listening ☐ Persistence ☐ Flexibility ☐ Practice

Other ☐ _____

## Goals for the Year

_____

_____

_____

_____

## I promise to improve on:

_____

_____

_____

Notes _____

_____

_____

I love my club because

_____

_____

Favorite famous gymnast _____

Favorite coach _____

My Gymnastics Friends _____

_____

Funniest _____

Chattiest _____

Bravest _____

## This is my favorite leotard

Color

_____

Design

_____

# Class Schedule

# Safety Tip Sheet

- Always warm up and stretch before doing gymnastics.

- Only practice on padded floors, never on a hard surface.

- Mats should be placed under the equipment and properly secured at all times.

- Have a coach spotting for all new or difficult skills.

- Let the coach know if you are uncomfortable with a gymnastic move. If the coach isn't supportive, tell a parent or an administrator.

- Never try a stunt at a game or competition that you haven't practiced many times.

- Follow gym rules for your club such as:
  - 1 person on a trampoline at a time
  - when jumping into a foam pit, land on feet, bottom, or back; no diving headfirst or landing on the knees
  - 1 person at a time on the equipment (such as uneven bars, rings, or balance beam)
  - No training alone
  - Wear gymnastic clothes that won't get caught on any of the equipment.
  - No jewelry
  - No gum chewing

- Stop training if you get hurt or feel pain. See a medical professional if injury persists over training sessions.

- Play different sports throughout the year to prevent overuse injuries.

- Know the team plan for emergencies.
  This includes calling 911 for a head, neck, or back injury and NOT moving the hurt gymnast.

# Word Search

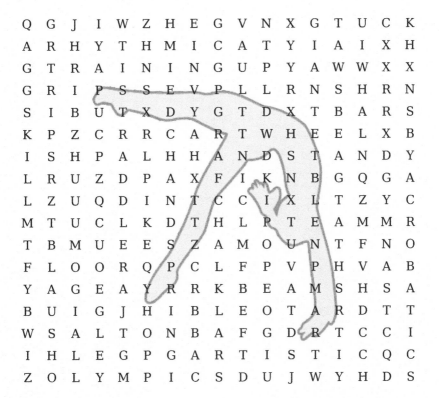

```
Q G J I W Z H E G V N X G T U C K
A R H Y T H M I C A T Y I A I X H
G T R A I N I N G U P Y A W W X X
G R I P S S E V P L L R N S H R N
S I B U T X D Y G T D X T B A R S
K P Z C R R C A R T W H E E L X B
I S H P A L H H A N D S T A N D Y
L R U Z D P A X F I K N B G Q G A
L Z U Q D I N T C C I X L T Z Y C
M T U C L K D T H L P T E A M M R
T B M U E E S Z A M O U N T F N O
F L O O R Q P C L F P V P H V A B
Y A G E A Y R R K B E A M S H S A
B U I G J H I B L E O T A R D T T
W S A L T O N B A F G D R T C C I
I H L E G P G A R T I S T I C Q C
Z O L Y M P I C S D U J W Y H D S
```

HANDSPRING, HANDSTAND, CHALK,
CARTWHEEL, TEAM, RHYTHMIC, LEOTARD,
GIANT, RIPS, ACROBATICS, FLOOR, STRADDLE,
VAULT, SALTO, MOUNT, KIP, OLYMPICS,
TRAINING, TUCK, PIKE, GYMNAST, ARTISTIC,
BEAM, GRIPS, BARS, SKILL

# GOAL TRACKER

Goal:

Action Steps:

1.

2.

3.

By Date:

Goal:

Action Steps:

1.

2.

3.

By Date:

Goal:

Action Steps:

1.

2.

3.

By Date:

Goal:

Action Steps:

1.

2.

3.

By Date:

Progress Notes:

# GOAL TRACKER

## Goal:

### Action Steps:

1.

2.

3.

By Date:

## Goal:

### Action Steps:

1.

2.

3.

By Date:

## Goal:

### Action Steps:

1.

2.

3.

By Date:

## Goal:

### Action Steps:

1.

2.

3.

By Date:

### Progress Notes:

# GOAL TRACKER

**Goal:**

**Action Steps:**

1.

2.

3.

**By Date:**

**Goal:**

**Action Steps:**

1.

2.

3.

**By Date:**

**Goal:**

**Action Steps:**

1.

2.

3.

**By Date:**

**Goal:**

**Action Steps:**

1.

2.

3.

**By Date:**

**Progress Notes:**

# GOAL TRACKER

Goal: _____

_____

Action Steps: _____

1. _____

2. _____

3. _____

By Date: _____

Goal: _____

_____

Action Steps: _____

1. _____

2. _____

3. _____

By Date: _____

Goal: _____

_____

Action Steps: _____

1. _____

2. _____

3. _____

By Date: _____

Goal: _____

_____

Action Steps: _____

1. _____

2. _____

3. _____

By Date: _____

Progress Notes: _____

_____

_____

_____

_____

_____

# Notes

Week ........

*Your limitation—
it's only your imagination.*

Monday

_____

Tuesday

_____

Wednesday

_____

Thursday

_____

Friday

_____

Saturday

_____

Sunday

_____

Priorities

To Do

★
★
★
★

Notes

# My Training Week

Coach Name: _____

Hours Trained: _____

Achievements: _____

How I felt  😞  🙂  😐  🙂  😀

Conditioning notes

| Skill: | Rep: |
|--------|------|
|        |      |
|        |      |
|        |      |
|        |      |

Coach Said:

Best thing this week:

I am
grateful for

week ........

*Sometimes later becomes never. Do it Now.*

Monday
_____

Tuesday
_____

Wednesday
_____

Thursday
_____

Friday
_____

Saturday
_____

Sunday
_____

Priorities

To Do
- ★
- ★
- ★
- ★

Notes

# My Training Week

Coach Name: _____

Hours Trained: _____

Achievements: _____

How I felt    ☹   🙂   😐   🙂   😀

Conditioning notes

| Skill: | Rep: |
|--------|------|
|        |      |
|        |      |
|        |      |
|        |      |
|        |      |

Coach Said:

Best thing this week:

*I am grateful for*

Week ............

*Great things never come from comfort zones.*

Monday

_____

Tuesday

_____

Wednesday

_____

Thursday

_____

Friday

_____

Saturday

_____

Sunday

_____

Priorities

To Do

★

★

★

★

Notes

# My Training Week

Coach Name: _____

Hours Trained: _____

Achievements: _____

How I felt  ☹ 🙂 😐 🙂 😄

Conditioning notes

| Skill: | Rep: |
|--------|------|
|        |      |
|        |      |
|        |      |
|        |      |

Coach Said:

Best thing this week:

*I am grateful for*

Week ◆◆◆◆◆◆◆◆◆

*Dream it. Wish it. Do it.*

Monday

_____

Tuesday

_____

Wednesday

Thursday

_____

Friday

_____

Saturday

_____

Sunday

_____

Priorities

To Do

- ★
- ★
- ★
- ★

Notes

# My Training Week

Coach Name: _____

Hours Trained: _____

Achievements: _____

How I felt  ☹ 😐 😐 🙂 😃

Conditioning notes

| Skill: | Rep: |
| --- | --- |
| | |
| | |
| | |
| | |
| | |

Coach Said:

Best thing this week:

I am grateful for

# Week ........

*Success doesn't just find you. You have to go out & get it.*

**Monday**

**Tuesday**

**Wednesday**

**Thursday**

**Friday**

**Saturday**

**Sunday**

## Priorities

## To Do

- ★
- ★
- ★
- ★

## Notes

# My Training Week

Coach Name: _____

Hours Trained: _____

Achievements: _____

How I felt    ☹  🙂  😐  🙂  😀

Conditioning notes

| Skill: | Rep: |
|--------|------|
|        |      |
|        |      |
|        |      |
|        |      |

Coach Said:

Best thing this week:

*I am grateful for*

Week .........

Monday

_____

Tuesday

_____

Wednesday

_____

Thursday

_____

Friday

_____

Saturday

_____

Sunday

_____

*Dream bigger. Do bigger.*

Priorities

To Do

- ★
- ★
- ★
- ★

Notes

# My Training Week

Coach Name: _____

Hours Trained: _____

Achievements: _____

How I felt  ☹ 😕 😐 🙂 😃

Conditioning notes

| Skill: | Rep: |
|--------|------|
|        |      |
|        |      |
|        |      |
|        |      |

Coach Said:

Best thing this week:

I am
grateful for

# Week ••••••••

Monday

_____

Tuesday

_____

Wednesday

_____

Thursday

_____

Friday

_____

Saturday

_____

Sunday

_____

Priorities

To Do

★

★

★

★

Notes

# My Training Week

Coach Name: _____

Hours Trained: _____

Achievements: _____

How I felt    (☹)  (☺)  (😐)  (🙂)  (😀)

Conditioning notes

| Skill: | Rep: |
|--------|------|
|        |      |
|        |      |
|        |      |
|        |      |

Coach Said:

Best thing this week:

*I am grateful for*

Week ..........

*Wake up with determination.*
*Go to bed with satisfaction.*

Monday
_____

Tuesday
_____

Wednesday
_____

Thursday
_____

Friday
_____

Saturday
_____

Sunday
_____

Priorities

To Do
★
★
★
★

Notes

# My Training Week

Coach Name: _____

Hours Trained: _____

Achievements: _____

How I felt  ☹ 🙁 😐 🙂 😀

Conditioning notes

| Skill: | Rep: |
| --- | --- |
|  |  |
|  |  |
|  |  |
|  |  |

Coach Said:

Best thing this week:

*I am grateful for*

Week ...........

*Do something today that your future self will thank you for.*

Monday

_____

Tuesday

_____

Wednesday

_____

Thursday

_____

Friday

_____

Saturday

_____

Sunday

_____

Priorities

To Do

★

★

★

★

Notes

# My Training Week

Coach Name: _____

Hours Trained: _____

Achievements: _____

How I felt  ☹ 🙁 😐 🙂 😃

Conditioning notes

| Skill: | Rep: |
|--------|------|
|        |      |
|        |      |
|        |      |
|        |      |

Coach Said:

Best thing this week:

*I am grateful for*

*Little things make big days.*

# Week ◆◆◆◆◆◆◆

Monday
_____

Tuesday
_____

Wednesday
_____

Thursday
_____

Friday
_____

Saturday
_____

Sunday
_____

Priorities

To Do
★
★
★
★

Notes

# My Training Week

Coach Name: _____

Hours Trained: _____

Achievements: _____

How I felt  ☹  🙂  😐  🙂  😄

Conditioning notes

| Skill: | Rep: |
|--------|------|
|        |      |
|        |      |
|        |      |
|        |      |

Coach Said:

Best thing this week:

I am
grateful for

# Week ···········

*It's going to be hard – but hard doesn't mean impossible.*

Monday

_____

Tuesday

_____

Wednesday

_____

Thursday

_____

Friday

_____

Saturday

_____

Sunday

_____

## Priorities

## To Do

- ★
- ★
- ★
- ★

## Notes

# My Training Week

Coach Name: _____

Hours Trained: _____

Achievements: _____

How I felt  ☹ 😐 😐 🙂 😄

Conditioning notes

| Skill: | Rep: |
|--------|------|
|        |      |
|        |      |
|        |      |
|        |      |
|        |      |

Coach Said:

Best thing this week:

*I am grateful for*

Week ○●●●●●●●●

*Don't wait for opportunity — create it.*

Monday

Tuesday

Wednesday

Thursday

Friday

Saturday

Sunday

### Priorities

### To Do

- ★
- ★
- ★
- ★

### Notes

# My Training Week

Coach Name: _____

Hours Trained: _____

Achievements: _____

How I felt  ☹ ☺ 😐 ☺ 😀

Conditioning notes

| Skill: | Rep: |
|--------|------|
|        |      |
|        |      |
|        |      |
|        |      |

Coach Said:

Best thing this week:

*I am grateful for*

# Week ••••••••

*Sometimes we're tested not to show our weaknesses, but to discover our strengths.*

Monday
_____

Tuesday
_____

Wednesday
_____

Thursday
_____

Friday
_____

Saturday
_____

Sunday
_____

## Priorities

## To Do

★

★

★

★

## Notes

# My Training Week

Coach Name: _____

Hours Trained: _____

Achievements: _____

How I felt  ☹ ☺ 😐 ☺ 😀

Conditioning notes

| Skill: | Rep: |
|--------|------|
|        |      |
|        |      |
|        |      |
|        |      |

Coach Said:

Best thing this week:

*I am grateful for*

# Week ........

*The key to success is to focus on goals, not obstacles.*

**Monday**

_____

**Tuesday**

_____

**Wednesday**

_____

**Thursday**

_____

**Friday**

_____

**Saturday**

_____

**Sunday**

_____

## Priorities

## To Do

- ★
- ★
- ★
- ★

## Notes

# My Training Week

Coach Name: _____

Hours Trained: _____

Achievements: _____

How I felt   ☹ 😕 😐 🙂 😀

Conditioning notes

| Skill: | Rep: |
|--------|------|
|        |      |
|        |      |
|        |      |
|        |      |

Coach Said:

Best thing this week:

I am
grateful for

Week ●●●●●●●●●

Dream it. Believe it.
Build it.

Monday
_____

Tuesday
_____

Wednesday
_____

Thursday
_____

Friday
_____

Saturday
_____

Sunday
_____

Priorities

To Do

★

★

★

★

Notes

# My Training Week

Coach Name: _____

Hours Trained: _____

Achievements: _____

How I felt  ☹ ☺ 😐 ☺ 😄

Conditioning notes

| Skill: | Rep: |
|--------|------|
|        |      |
|        |      |
|        |      |
|        |      |

Coach Said:

Best thing this week:

*I am grateful for*

Week ●◆◆◆◆◆◆◆

*You've come so far –
don't quit now.*

Priorities

Monday

_____

Tuesday

_____

Wednesday

_____

To Do

★

★

★

★

Thursday

_____

Friday

_____

Notes

Saturday

_____

Sunday

_____

# My Training Week

Coach Name: _____

Hours Trained: _____

Achievements: _____

How I felt  ☹ 😕 😐 🙂 😃

Conditioning notes

| Skill: | Rep: |
| --- | --- |
|  |  |
|  |  |
|  |  |
|  |  |

Coach Said:

Best thing this week:

I am grateful for

Week ........

*To reach your goals, you must grab on with both hands.*

Monday
_____

Tuesday
_____

Wednesday
_____

Thursday
_____

Friday
_____

Saturday
_____

Sunday
_____

Priorities

To Do
- ★
- ★
- ★
- ★

Notes

# My Training Week

Coach Name: _____

Hours Trained: _____

Achievements: _____

How I felt    ☹  😐  😐  🙂  😄

Conditioning notes

| Skill: | Rep: |
|--------|------|
|        |      |
|        |      |
|        |      |
|        |      |

Coach Said:

Best thing this week:

I am
grateful for

Week ..........

*You are your only limit.*

Monday
_____

Tuesday
_____

Wednesday
_____

Thursday
_____

Friday
_____

Saturday
_____

Sunday
_____

Priorities

To Do

★

★

★

★

Notes

# My Training Week

Coach Name: _____

Hours Trained: _____

Achievements: _____

How I felt    ☹ 😐 😐 🙂 😃

Conditioning notes

| Skill: | Rep: |
|--------|------|
|        |      |
|        |      |
|        |      |
|        |      |
|        |      |

Coach Said:

Best thing this week:

*I am grateful for*

*Play like you are in first.*
*Train like you are in second.*

# Week ........

## Monday

_____

## Tuesday

_____

## Wednesday

_____

## Thursday

_____

## Friday

_____

## Saturday

_____

## Sunday

_____

### Priorities

### To Do

★
★
★
★

### Notes

# My Training Week

Coach Name: _____

Hours Trained: _____

Achievements: _____

How I felt ☹ 😕 😐 🙂 😊

Conditioning notes

| Skill: | Rep: |
|--------|------|
|        |      |
|        |      |
|        |      |
|        |      |

Coach Said:

Best thing this week:

*I am grateful for*

*I can and I will.*

# Week ⬥⬥⬥⬥⬥⬥⬥⬥⬥

Monday

_____

Tuesday

_____

Wednesday

_____

Thursday

_____

Friday

_____

Saturday

_____

Sunday

_____

## Priorities

## To Do

★

★

★

★

## Notes

# My Training Week

Coach Name: _____

Hours Trained: _____

Achievements: _____

How I felt  😦 😕 😐 🙂 😃

Conditioning notes

| Skill: | Rep: |
|--------|------|
|        |      |
|        |      |
|        |      |
|        |      |

Coach Said:

Best thing this week:

*I am grateful for*

Week ••••••••

*It never gets easier — you just get better.*

Monday
_____

Tuesday
_____

Wednesday
_____

Thursday
_____

Friday
_____

Saturday
_____

Sunday
_____

Priorities

To Do

★

★

★

★

Notes

# My Training Week

Coach Name: _____

Hours Trained: _____

Achievements: _____

How I felt 😦 😐 😐 🙂 😄

Conditioning notes

| Skill: | Rep: |
|--------|------|
|        |      |
|        |      |
|        |      |
|        |      |

Coach Said:

Best thing this week:

*I am grateful for*

Week ●●●●●●●●●●

*Pain is temporary –
Greatness is forever.*

Monday
_____

Tuesday
_____

Wednesday
_____

Thursday
_____

Friday
_____

Saturday
_____

Sunday
_____

Priorities

To Do

★
★
★
★

Notes

# My Training Week

Coach Name: _____

Hours Trained: _____

Achievements: _____

How I felt ☹ 😐 😐 🙂 😀

Conditioning notes

| Skill: | Rep: |
|--------|------|
|  |  |
|  |  |
|  |  |
|  |  |
|  |  |

Coach Said:

Best thing this week:

*I am grateful for*

# Week

*You are stronger than you think.*

Monday

Tuesday

Wednesday

Thursday

Friday

Saturday

Sunday

## Priorities

## To Do

- ★
- ★
- ★
- ★

## Notes

# My Training Week

Coach Name: _____

Hours Trained: _____

Achievements: _____

How I felt  ☹ 😕 😐 🙂 😀

Conditioning notes

| Skill: | Rep: |
| --- | --- |
|  |  |
|  |  |
|  |  |
|  |  |

Coach Said:

Best thing this week:

*I am grateful for*

Week ........

*If you don't leap you will never know what its like to fly.*

Monday
_____

Tuesday
_____

Wednesday
_____

Thursday
_____

Friday
_____

Saturday
_____

Sunday
_____

Priorities

To Do
- ★
- ★
- ★
- ★

Notes

# My Training Week

Coach Name: _____

Hours Trained: _____

Achievements: _____

How I felt  ☹ ☹ 😐 🙂 😄

Conditioning notes

| Skill: | Rep: |
|--------|------|
|        |      |
|        |      |
|        |      |
|        |      |

Coach Said:

Best thing this week:

*I am grateful for*

Week ............

*To be a champion you have to train like a champion.*

Monday

_____

Tuesday

_____

Wednesday

_____

Thursday

_____

Friday

_____

Saturday

_____

Sunday

_____

Priorities

To Do

- ★
- ★
- ★
- ★

Notes

# My Training Week

Coach Name: _____

Hours Trained: _____

Achievements: _____

How I felt  ☹ 🙁 😐 🙂 😀

Conditioning notes

| Skill: | Rep: |
| --- | --- |
|  |  |
|  |  |
|  |  |
|  |  |
|  |  |

Coach Said:

Best thing this week:

*I am grateful for*

Week ......

*Don't practice until you get it right. Practice until you can't get it wrong.*

Monday
_____

Tuesday
_____

Wednesday
_____

Thursday
_____

Friday
_____

Saturday
_____

Sunday
_____

Priorities

To Do

★
★
★
★

Notes

# My Training Week

Coach Name: _____

Hours Trained: _____

Achievements: _____

How I felt  ☹ 😕 😐 🙂 😃

Conditioning notes

| Skill: | Rep: |
|--------|------|
|        |      |
|        |      |
|        |      |
|        |      |

Coach Said:

Best thing this week:

*I am grateful for*

Week .........

*Losers quit when they are tired. Winners quit when they have won.*

Monday
_____

Tuesday
_____

Wednesday
_____

Thursday
_____

Friday
_____

Saturday
_____

Sunday
_____

Priorities

To Do

- ★
- ★
- ★
- ★

Notes

# My Training Week

Coach Name: _____

Hours Trained: _____

Achievements: _____

How I felt  ☹ ☺ 😐 🙂 😃

Conditioning notes

| Skill: | Rep: |
|--------|------|
|        |      |
|        |      |
|        |      |
|        |      |

Coach Said:

Best thing this week:

*I am grateful for*

Week ••••••••••

*Take your dreams seriously.*

Monday

_____

Tuesday

_____

Wednesday

_____

Thursday

_____

Friday

_____

Saturday

_____

Sunday

_____

Priorities

To Do

★
★
★
★

Notes

# My Training Week

Coach Name: _____

Hours Trained: _____

Achievements: _____

How I felt 🙁 🙂 😐 🙂 😃

Conditioning notes

| Skill: | Rep: |
|--------|------|
|        |      |
|        |      |
|        |      |
|        |      |

Coach Said:

Best thing this week:

*I am grateful for*

Week ----------

*Forget the mistake – remember the lesson.*

Monday

_____

Tuesday

_____

Wednesday

_____

Thursday

_____

Friday

_____

Saturday

_____

Sunday

_____

Priorities

To Do

★
★
★
★

Notes

# My Training Week

Coach Name: _____

Hours Trained: _____

Achievements: _____

How I felt  ☹  🙁  😐  🙂  😀

Conditioning notes

| Skill: | Rep: |
|--------|------|
|        |      |
|        |      |
|        |      |
|        |      |

Coach Said:

Best thing this week:

*I am grateful for*

Week ••••••••••

*Work hard - dream big.*

Monday

_____

Tuesday

_____

Wednesday

_____

Thursday

_____

Friday

_____

Saturday

_____

Sunday

_____

Priorities

To Do

★

★

★

★

Notes

# My Training Week

Coach Name: _____

Hours Trained: _____

Achievements: _____

How I felt  ☹ 🙂 😐 🙂 😄

Conditioning notes

| Skill: | Rep: |
|--------|------|
|        |      |
|        |      |
|        |      |
|        |      |

Coach Said:

Best thing this week:

*I am grateful for*

Week ·········

*Make it happen –
Shock everyone.*

Monday

_____

Tuesday

_____

Wednesday

_____

Thursday

_____

Friday

_____

Saturday

_____

Sunday

_____

Priorities

To Do

★
★
★
★

Notes

# My Training Week

Coach Name: _____

Hours Trained: _____

Achievements: _____

How I felt     ☹️    😕    😐    🙂    😄

Conditioning notes

| Skill: | Rep: |
|--------|------|
|        |      |
|        |      |
|        |      |
|        |      |
|        |      |

Coach Said:            Best thing this week:

*I am grateful for*

Week .........

Monday
_____

Tuesday
_____

Wednesday
_____

Thursday
_____

Friday
_____

Saturday
_____

Sunday
_____

Priorities

To Do

★
★
★
★

Notes

# My Training Week

Coach Name: _____

Hours Trained: _____

Achievements: _____

How I felt   ☹ 😕 😐 🙂 😄

Conditioning notes

| Skill: | Rep: |
|--------|------|
|        |      |
|        |      |
|        |      |
|        |      |
|        |      |

Coach Said:

Best thing this week:

I am
grateful for

Week ............

*Work Hard, Hussle, Grind.*

Monday
_____

Tuesday
_____

Wednesday
_____

Thursday
_____

Friday
_____

Saturday
_____

Sunday
_____

Priorities

To Do
- ★
- ★
- ★
- ★

Notes

# My Training Week

Coach Name: _____

Hours Trained: _____

Achievements: _____

How I felt  ☹ 🙂 😐 🙂 😄

Conditioning notes

| Skill: | Rep: |
| --- | --- |
|  |  |
|  |  |
|  |  |
|  |  |

Coach Said:

Best thing this week:

*I am grateful for*

*Be driven.*

Week ·········

Monday

_____

Tuesday

_____

Wednesday

_____

Thursday

_____

Friday

_____

Saturday

_____

Sunday

_____

Priorities

To Do

★

★

★

★

Notes

# My Training Week

Coach Name: _____

Hours Trained: _____

Achievements: _____

How I felt  ☹ 😕 😐 🙂 😃

Conditioning notes

| Skill: | Rep: |
| --- | --- |
|  |  |
|  |  |
|  |  |
|  |  |
|  |  |

Coach Said:

Best thing this week:

*I am grateful for*

*Be hungry.*

Week ....................

Monday

_____

Tuesday

_____

Wednesday

_____

Thursday

_____

Friday

_____

Saturday

_____

Sunday

_____

Priorities

To Do

★

★

★

★

Notes

# My Training Week

Coach Name: _____

Hours Trained: _____

Achievements: _____

How I felt  ☹ 🙁 😐 🙂 😀

Conditioning notes

| Skill: | Rep: |
|--------|------|
|        |      |
|        |      |
|        |      |
|        |      |

Coach Said:

Best thing this week:

I am grateful for

Be positive.

Week .............

Monday

Tuesday

Wednesday

Thursday

Friday

Saturday

Sunday

Priorities

To Do

★

★

★

★

Notes

# My Training Week

Coach Name: _____

Hours Trained: _____

Achievements: _____

How I felt  ☹ 🙁 😐 🙂 😃

Conditioning notes

| Skill: | Rep: |
|--------|------|
|        |      |
|        |      |
|        |      |
|        |      |

Coach Said:                    Best thing this week:

*I am grateful for*

# Ode to the Beam Queen

I tumble high
I fall, I sigh

I soar, I spin
I slip, I cry

One hundred times
and one time more,
Practice, practice 'til you're sore

To seek perfection on the beam
Is so much harder than it might seem

When you feel like you must give up on it
This is the very time you must not quit

By Fiona Gamble (Former gymnast and dreamer)

# Go With the Flow

I love to fly, to tumble and prance
To spin and turn and gracefully dance
Some moves are hard and take some time
With practice I know success can be mine

I stretch and I stretch, I repeat to the beat
I dream I am dancing as I walk down the street
To win a big meet is my hope and my dream
Although my gym coach says it's not all it seems

Most of all I am happy to go with the flow
To move with the music and see where I go
To be filled with the moves and feel free as can be
This is the most important to me

By Fiona Gamble (Former gymnast and dreamer)

Week ........

*It's not about how good you are, but how bad you want it.*

Monday

Tuesday

Wednesday

Thursday

Friday

Saturday

Sunday

Priorities

To Do

- ★
- ★
- ★
- ★

Notes

# My Training Week

Coach Name: _____

Hours Trained: _____

Achievements: _____

How I felt  ☹ 🙁 😐 🙂 😀

Conditioning notes

| Skill: | Rep: |
|--------|------|
|        |      |
|        |      |
|        |      |
|        |      |

Coach Said:

Best thing this week:

I am
grateful for

Week ••••••••••

*You only see obstacles when you take your eye off the goal.*

Monday

Tuesday

Wednesday

Thursday

Friday

Saturday

Sunday

Priorities

To Do

★

★

★

★

Notes

# My Training Week

Coach Name: _____

Hours Trained: _____

Achievements: _____

How I felt  ☹  🙁  😐  🙂  😃

Conditioning notes

| Skill: | Rep: |
| --- | --- |
|  |  |
|  |  |
|  |  |
|  |  |

Coach Said:

Best thing this week:

*I am grateful for*

Week ‧‧‧‧‧‧‧‧‧

Let your mistakes make you better not bitter.

Monday

_____

Tuesday

_____

Wednesday

_____

Thursday

_____

Friday

_____

Saturday

_____

Sunday

_____

Priorities

To Do

★
★
★
★

Notes

# My Training Week

Coach Name: _____

Hours Trained: _____

Achievements: _____

How I felt  ☹ 🙁 😐 🙂 😀

Conditioning notes

| Skill: | Rep: |
|--------|------|
|        |      |
|        |      |
|        |      |
|        |      |
|        |      |

Coach Said:

Best thing this week:

*I am grateful for*

# Week ..........

*Practice like you've never Won.
Play like you've never Lost.*

## Monday

_____

## Tuesday

_____

## Wednesday

_____

## Thursday

_____

## Friday

_____

## Saturday

_____

## Sunday

_____

## Priorities

## To Do

★

★

★

★

## Notes

# My Training Week

Coach Name: _____

Hours Trained: _____

Achievements: _____

How I felt    ☹ ☺ 😐 ☺ 😄

Conditioning notes

| Skill: | Rep: |
|--------|------|
|        |      |
|        |      |
|        |      |
|        |      |

Coach Said:

Best thing this week:

I am
grateful for

Week ·····

*Hard work makes things look easy.*

Monday
_____

Tuesday
_____

Wednesday
_____

Thursday
_____

Friday
_____

Saturday
_____

Sunday
_____

Priorities

To Do
★
★
★
★

Notes

# My Training Week

Coach Name: _____

Hours Trained: _____

Achievements: _____

How I felt  ☹ ☺ 😐 ☺ 😃

Conditioning notes

| Skill: | Rep: |
|--------|------|
|        |      |
|        |      |
|        |      |
|        |      |
|        |      |

Coach Said:

Best thing this week:

*I am grateful for*

Week ●●●●●●●●●●

*Sometimes you win, sometimes you learn.*

Monday

_____

Tuesday

_____

Wednesday

_____

Thursday

_____

Friday

_____

Saturday

_____

Sunday

_____

Priorities

To Do

★

★

★

★

Notes

# My Training Week

Coach Name: _____

Hours Trained: _____

Achievements: _____

How I felt    ☹ ☺ 😐 ☺ 😄

Conditioning notes

| Skill: | Rep: |
|--------|------|
|        |      |
|        |      |
|        |      |
|        |      |

Coach Said:

Best thing this week:

I am
grateful for

Week •••••••••

Be so good that they can't ignore you.

Monday

_____

Tuesday

_____

Wednesday

_____

Thursday

_____

Friday

_____

Saturday

_____

Sunday

_____

Priorities

To Do

★
★
★
★

Notes

# My Training Week

Coach Name: _____

Hours Trained: _____

Achievements: _____

How I felt 😞 😐 😐 🙂 😄

Conditioning notes

| Skill: | Rep: |
|--------|------|
|        |      |
|        |      |
|        |      |
|        |      |

Coach Said:

Best thing this week:

I am
grateful for

Week ••••••••••

Monday

_____

Tuesday

_____

Wednesday

_____

Thursday

_____

Friday

_____

Saturday

_____

Sunday

_____

Priorities

To Do

★

★

★

★

Notes

# My Training Week

Coach Name: _____

Hours Trained: _____

Achievements: _____

How I felt  ☹ 🙂 😐 🙂 😃

## Conditioning notes

| Skill: | Rep: |
|--------|------|
|        |      |
|        |      |
|        |      |
|        |      |

Coach Said:

Best thing this week:

*I am grateful for*

Week ........

*Don't let anyone ever dull your sparkle.*

Monday

_____

Tuesday

_____

Wednesday

_____

Thursday

_____

Friday

_____

Saturday

_____

Sunday

_____

Priorities

To Do

- ★
- ★
- ★
- ★

Notes

# My Training Week

Coach Name: _____

Hours Trained: _____

Achievements: _____

How I felt  ☹  🙁  😐  🙂  😀

Conditioning notes

| Skill: | Rep: |
|--------|------|
|        |      |
|        |      |
|        |      |
|        |      |
|        |      |

Coach Said:

Best thing this week:

*I am
grateful for*

# Week ·········

Monday

_____

Tuesday

_____

Wednesday

_____

Thursday

_____

Friday

_____

Saturday

_____

Sunday

_____

Priorities

To Do

★

★

★

★

Notes

# My Training Week

Coach Name: _____

Hours Trained: _____

Achievements: _____

How I felt   ☹ 😐 😐 🙂 😃

Conditioning notes

| Skill: | Rep: |
|--------|------|
|        |      |
|        |      |
|        |      |
|        |      |

Coach Said:

Best thing this week:

*I am grateful for*

Week ━━━━━━━━━

*You don't have to see the whole staircase to take the first step.*

Monday

Tuesday

Wednesday

Thursday

Friday

Saturday

Sunday

Priorities

To Do

- ★
- ★
- ★
- ★

Notes

# My Training Week

Coach Name: _____

Hours Trained: _____

Achievements: _____

How I felt  😦 😐 😐 🙂 😃

Conditioning notes

| Skill: | Rep: |
|--------|------|
|        |      |
|        |      |
|        |      |
|        |      |

Coach Said:

Best thing this week:

*I am grateful for*

Be a light to the world.

Week ............

Monday

_____

Tuesday

_____

Wednesday

_____

Thursday

_____

Friday

_____

Saturday

_____

Sunday

_____

Priorities

To Do

★

★

★

★

Notes

# My Training Week

Coach Name: _____

Hours Trained: _____

Achievements: _____

How I felt ☹ 😐 😐 🙂 😀

Conditioning notes

| Skill: | Rep: |
|--------|------|
|        |      |
|        |      |
|        |      |
|        |      |

Coach Said:

Best thing this week:

*I am grateful for*

Week ••••••••••

There is always room to improve. Always.

Monday
_____

Tuesday
_____

Wednesday
_____

Thursday
_____

Friday
_____

Saturday
_____

Sunday
_____

Priorities

To Do
★
★
★
★

Notes

# My Training Week

Coach Name: _____

Hours Trained: _____

Achievements: _____

How I felt   ☹ ☺ ☺ ☺ ☺

Conditioning notes

| Skill: | Rep: |
|--------|------|
|        |      |
|        |      |
|        |      |
|        |      |

Coach Said:

Best thing this week:

*I am grateful for*

Week ...........

*The pain you feel today is the strength you feel tomorrow.*

**Monday**

**Tuesday**

**Wednesday**

**Thursday**

**Friday**

**Saturday**

**Sunday**

**Priorities**

**To Do**

- ★
- ★
- ★
- ★

**Notes**

# My Training Week

Coach Name: _____

Hours Trained: _____

Achievements: _____

How I felt  ☹ ☹ 😐 🙂 😃

Conditioning notes

| Skill: | Rep: |
|--------|------|
|        |      |
|        |      |
|        |      |
|        |      |

Coach Said:

Best thing this week:

*I am grateful for*

Week ·•◆•◆•◆•◆•◆•

*You only fail when you stop trying.*

Monday

_____

Tuesday

_____

Wednesday

_____

Thursday

_____

Friday

_____

Saturday

_____

Sunday

_____

Priorities

To Do

- ★
- ★
- ★
- ★

Notes

# My Training Week

Coach Name: _____

Hours Trained: _____

Achievements: _____

How I felt  ☹ 🙁 😐 🙂 😃

Conditioning notes

| Skill: | Rep: |
|--------|------|
|        |      |
|        |      |
|        |      |
|        |      |

Coach Said:

Best thing this week:

I am grateful for

Week ●◆●◆●◆●◆●◆

*Without risk there is no reward.*

Monday

_____

Tuesday

_____

Wednesday

_____

Thursday

_____

Friday

_____

Saturday

_____

Sunday

_____

Priorities

To Do

★

★

★

★

Notes

# My Training Week

Coach Name: _____

Hours Trained: _____

Achievements: _____

How I felt  😞  🙂  😐  🙂  😀

Conditioning notes

| Skill: | Rep: |
|--------|------|
|        |      |
|        |      |
|        |      |
|        |      |

Coach Said:

Best thing this week:

I am
grateful for

# My Meets

Meet: _____

Level: _____

**_Vault_**    Score [    ]    Place [    ]

How I felt  😦  🙂  😐  🙂  😄

**_Bars_**    Score [    ]    Place [    ]

How I felt  😦  🙂  😐  🙂  😄

**_Beam_**    Score [    ]    Place [    ]

How I felt  😦  🙂  😐  🙂  😄

**_Floor_**    Score [    ]    Place [    ]

How I felt  😦  🙂  😐  🙂  😄

Notes _____
_____
_____

# My Meets

Meet: _____

Level: _____

**Vault**    Score [    ]    Place [    ]

How I felt   😖 🙂 😐 😊 😄

**Bars**    Score [    ]    Place [    ]

How I felt   😖 🙂 😐 😊 😄

**Beam**    Score [    ]    Place [    ]

How I felt   😖 🙂 😐 😊 😄

**Floor**    Score [    ]    Place [    ]

How I felt   😖 🙂 😐 😊 😄

Notes _____

_____

_____

 # My Meets

Meet: _____

Level: _____

## Vault
Score ☐   Place ☐

How I felt  ☹ 😕 😐 🙂 😄

## Bars
Score ☐   Place ☐

How I felt  ☹ 😕 😐 🙂 😄

## Beam
Score ☐   Place ☐

How I felt  ☹ 😕 😐 🙂 😄

## Floor
Score ☐   Place ☐

How I felt  ☹ 😕 😐 🙂 😄

Notes _____
_____
_____

 # My Meets

Meet: _____

Level: _____

## Vault
Score [ ]   Place [ ]

How I felt  😦 🙂 😐 😊 😁

## Bars
Score [ ]   Place [ ]

How I felt  😦 🙂 😐 😊 😁

## Beam
Score [ ]   Place [ ]

How I felt  😦 🙂 😐 😊 😁

## Floor
Score [ ]   Place [ ]

How I felt  😦 🙂 😐 😊 😁

Notes _____
_____
_____

 # My Meets

Meet: _____

Level: _____

## Vault
Score [ ]  Place [ ]

How I felt  😦  🙂  😐  🙂  😄

## Bars
Score [ ]  Place [ ]

How I felt  😦  🙂  😐  🙂  😄

## Beam
Score [ ]  Place [ ]

How I felt  😦  🙂  😐  🙂  😄

## Floor
Score [ ]  Place [ ]

How I felt  😦  🙂  😐  🙂  😄

Notes _____

_____

_____

 # My Meets

Meet: _____

Level: _____

## _Vault_  Score [          ]     Place [      ]

How I felt  ☹ ☺ 😐 🙂 😀

## _Bars_  Score [          ]     Place [      ]

How I felt  ☹ ☺ 😐 🙂 😀

## _Beam_  Score [          ]     Place [      ]

How I felt  ☹ ☺ 😐 🙂 😀

## _Floor_  Score [          ]     Place [      ]

How I felt  ☹ ☺ 😐 🙂 😀

Notes _____

_____

_____

# My Meets

Meet: _____

Level: _____

_Vault_    Score [    ]    Place [    ]

How I felt   😞  😊  😐  🙂  😃

_Bars_    Score [    ]    Place [    ]

How I felt   😞  😊  😐  🙂  😃

_Beam_    Score [    ]    Place [    ]

How I felt   😞  😊  😐  🙂  😃

_Floor_    Score [    ]    Place [    ]

How I felt   😞  😊  😐  🙂  😃

Notes _____

_____

_____

 # My Meets

Meet: _____

Level: _____

## Vault    Score [    ]    Place [    ]

How I felt    😟  😊  😐  🙂  😃

## Bars    Score [    ]    Place [    ]

How I felt    😟  😊  😐  🙂  😃

## Beam    Score [    ]    Place [    ]

How I felt    😟  😊  😐  🙂  😃

## Floor    Score [    ]    Place [    ]

How I felt    😟  😊  😐  🙂  😃

Notes _____
_____
_____

 # My Meets

Meet: _____

Level: _____

## *Vault*    Score [    ]    Place [    ]

How I felt   😦  🙂  😐  🙂  😀

## *Bars*    Score [    ]    Place [    ]

How I felt   😦  🙂  😐  🙂  😀

## *Beam*    Score [    ]    Place [    ]

How I felt   😦  🙂  😐  🙂  😀

## *Floor*    Score [    ]    Place [    ]

How I felt   😦  🙂  😐  🙂  😀

Notes _____
_____
_____

# Notes

# Notes

# Notes

# Notes

# Notes

# Notes